WORLD LEADERS

POPE FRANCIS
LEADER OF THE CATHOLIC CHURCH

by Kelsey Jopp

FOCUS READERS

www.focusreaders.com

Focus Readers is distributed by North Star Editions:
sales@northstareditions.com | 888-417-0195

Produced for Focus Readers by Red Line Editorial.

Content Consultant: Dr. Kristy Nabhan-Warren, Elizabeth Kahl Figge Chair of Catholic Studies, University of Iowa

Photographs ©: Alessandra Tarantino/AP Images, cover, 1, 4–5; photofilippo66/Shutterstock Images, 6; Yury Dmitrienko/Shutterstock Images, 8–9; Peter Hermes Furian/Shutterstock Images, 10; Sergey Kohl/Shutterstock Images, 13; nortongo/Shutterstock Images, 15; Natacha Pisarenko/AP Images, 16–17; Franco Origlia/Getty Images News/Getty Images Europe, 18; duncan1890/iStockphoto, 21; Massimo Sambucetti/AP Images, 22–23; rglinsky/iStockphoto, 24; franckreporter/iStockphoto, 27; L'Osservatore Romano/AP Images, 28–29; mgallar/Shutterstock Images, 31; Rathaporn Nanthapreecha/Shutterstock Images, 33; Desmond Boylan/AP Images, 34–35; Drop of Light/Shutterstock Images, 36; Gregorio Borgia/AP Images, 38; Alexandros Michailidis/Shutterstock Images, 41; giulio napolitano/Shutterstock Images, 42–43; Red Line Editorial, 44

Library of Congress Cataloging-in-Publication Data
Library of Congress Cataloging-in-Publication Data is available on the Library of Congress website.

ISBN
978-1-64185-364-4 (hardcover)
978-1-64185-422-1 (paperback)
978-1-64185-538-9 (ebook pdf)
978-1-64185-480-1 (hosted ebook)

Printed in the United States of America
Mankato, MN
October, 2018

ABOUT THE AUTHOR

Kelsey Jopp is an editor, writer, and lifelong learner. She lives in Saint Paul, Minnesota, where she enjoys doing yoga and playing endless fetch with her sheltie, Teddy.

TABLE OF CONTENTS

CHAPTER 1

A NEW POPE

In July 2013, Pope Francis took a boat to Lampedusa, a small Italian island in the Mediterranean Sea. The journey was his first trip outside Rome, Italy, since becoming pope of the Roman Catholic Church in March. Residents of the island greeted him by waving caps and flags.

A few days before his visit, a boat filled with 165 **migrants** had reached the island. They had left their homes in Africa in search of better lives.

Pope Francis shakes the hands of migrants on the Italian island of Lampedusa.

▲ Many migrants traveled across the Mediterranean Sea in small boats.

Over the past decade, Lampedusa had become a main entry point into Europe. But the route from North Africa to Lampedusa was dangerous. Many migrants drowned or died from the cold. In fact, more than 80 percent of migrant deaths in the Mediterranean Sea happened on the way to the island.

Pope Francis planned his visit after hearing about the dangers migrants faced. He spoke to migrants who survived the trip and paid his respects to those who died. He also held Mass, the main worship service in the Catholic Church. Most of the migrants on the island were Muslims. Pope Francis wanted to encourage peace between Catholics, who practice Christianity, and Muslims, who practice Islam.

Pope Francis's visit served as a message to the world. He urged nations in Europe to help and welcome migrants. His visit also sent a message to the Catholic Church. It reminded Catholics of their responsibility to care for people in need. In the years to come, his agenda for change would both inspire and anger the world.

THINK ABOUT IT ◁

Pope Francis used his actions to send a message. What is one issue you care about? What action could you take to show that?

CHAPTER 2

THE HISTORY OF POPES

The term *pope* comes from the Greek word *pappas*, which means "father." This name reflects the pope's role as leader of the Roman Catholic Church. With 1.2 billion members, Catholicism is one of the largest religions in the world. The pope addresses problems affecting Catholics and guides their beliefs on religious issues. The pope also serves as the **bishop** of Rome. He is the head of Vatican City as well.

A statue of Peter, the first pope, stands in front of St. Peter's Basilica in Vatican City.

Vatican City is completely surrounded by the city of Rome. But it is a separate country that is ruled by the Catholic Church.

VATICAN CITY MAP

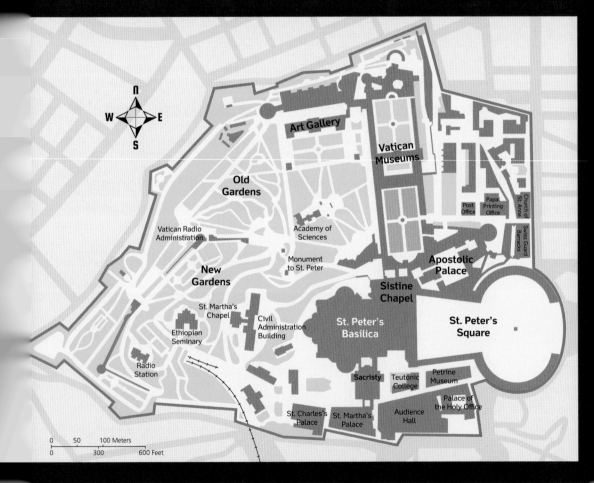

Throughout history, many popes have led the Catholic Church. Catholics believe the first pope was St. Peter. In the Bible, Peter was the leader of Jesus's 12 apostles, or followers. Catholics believe that Jesus chose Peter to lead the Church as well.

According to Catholic tradition, Peter left the city of Jerusalem after Jesus died. He traveled to Rome, where he worked to expand the Church. However, the emperor of Rome opposed this work. He had Peter killed in approximately 67 CE. Today, historians disagree about whether Peter actually went to Rome. Nevertheless, Rome became the center of the Catholic Church.

Since Peter, there have been more than 260 popes. The duties of the pope have changed over time. From the 700s until 1870, the pope ruled the Papal States. These states were territories in central Italy that belonged to the Catholic Church.

In 1870, the Italian government took over the Papal States. The Church and the government fought for control until 1929, when they signed the Lateran Treaty. The treaty recognized Vatican City as an independent country. The rest of the territory, including Rome, would be part of Italy.

Today, the pope oversees Vatican City and the worldwide Catholic Church. He has both political and religious duties. In Vatican City, he holds masses and greets the public each week. He also travels around the world to meet with political and religious leaders.

Within the Church, the pope appoints bishops and cardinals. Cardinals advise the pope about issues related to the Church. They also elect the new pope when the current pope dies.

To address major problems in the Church or change its teachings, the pope must arrange a

🔺 Bishops met in St. Peter's Basilica for the First Vatican Council, which lasted from 1869 to 1870.

council of bishops. Only two councils have met in the past 200 years. The First Vatican Council began in 1869 and gave greater authority to the pope. The Second Vatican Council met in 1962. This council changed the way the Church interacted with the world. It decided that Catholics could pray with other Christians. It also encouraged Catholics to have open discussions with people of other religions. Both councils helped guide the Church's future.

FOCUS ON
VATICAN CITY

Vatican City is an independent country located within the city of Rome. It has a population of approximately 800 people. It takes up an area of only 109 acres (44 hectares). In fact, it is the smallest country in the world.

Despite its small size, Vatican City has its own laws, police force, and bank. Its government is an absolute monarchy. This means the pope has supreme power. The pope **delegates** some power to a legislative body. This group helps make the country's laws. The pope appoints the members of this group. He also chooses who will lead it.

Vatican City does not have an official language. However, most communication is in Italian, English, French, German, or Spanish. Official documents in the Catholic Church are written in Latin.

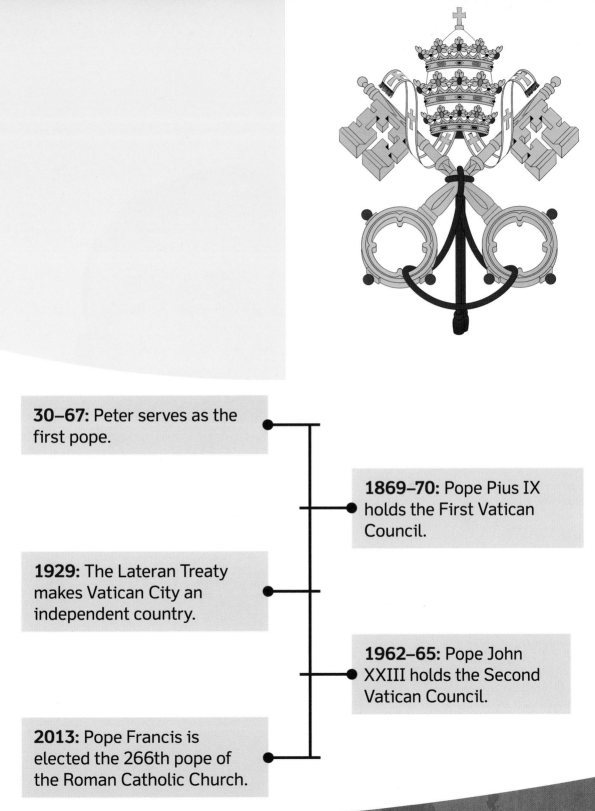

30–67: Peter serves as the first pope.

1869–70: Pope Pius IX holds the First Vatican Council.

1929: The Lateran Treaty makes Vatican City an independent country.

1962–65: Pope John XXIII holds the Second Vatican Council.

2013: Pope Francis is elected the 266th pope of the Roman Catholic Church.

CHAPTER 3

JORGE MARIO BERGOGLIO

Before he became the pope, Francis was known as Jorge Mario Bergoglio. Jorge was born in Argentina in 1936. However, his family was originally from Italy. Jorge's grandparents and father had left Italy in 1929. At that time, Italy was struggling financially. Jorge's grandparents, along with many other Italians, hoped to find better lives in Argentina.

Jorge Bergoglio stands in front of the flag of Argentina, the country where he was born.

Jorge Bergoglio (top row, second from left) and his family lived in Buenos Aires, Argentina, for many years.

When they arrived, businesses in Argentina were booming. But less than a year later, the Great Depression hit the United States. The Depression was a financial crisis that spread throughout the world. Within two years, Jorge's grandparents and father went broke. To make ends meet, they began selling goods on the streets.

Jorge grew up listening to stories of his family's time as migrants. These stories helped shape him as a leader. As pope, he would speak out about helping the poor and suffering.

Jorge's family influenced his life in other ways as well. In Italy, his grandmother Rosa had been very involved in both religion and politics. She had joined a group called Catholic Action. Its members protested Italian dictator Benito Mussolini. They thought he had too much power over the Catholic Church. Government leaders tried to keep Catholic Action from speaking out. One time, they closed down the hall where Rosa was supposed to speak. But she was not silenced. She spoke on top of a table in the street.

Rosa taught Jorge about Catholicism. She took him to Mass and showed him how to pray. She also taught him to have compassion. She believed Catholics should love everyone, no matter their religion.

Like his grandmother, Jorge became passionate about religion and politics. He was also interested in science. In high school, he studied food science and worked at a chemistry lab. But he wasn't sure what he wanted to do for a career.

The answer came one morning when he was 16 years old. Jorge was on his way to see friends when he passed a Catholic church. He felt an urge to go inside. So he went in and gave **confession** to a priest. This was something Jorge did often. But as he and the priest chatted afterward, a strange feeling came over Jorge. He knew he needed to become a priest.

> ## ➤ THINK ABOUT IT
>
> What values or practices are important to your family? Can you think of ways they have influenced your life?

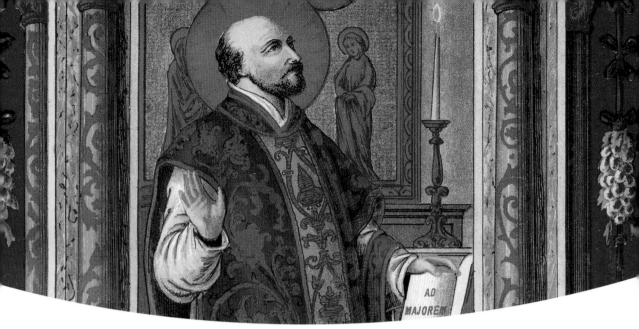

▲ A Spanish priest named Ignatius of Loyola founded the Society of Jesus in 1534.

Jorge Bergoglio began attending **seminary** three years later, in 1955. In 1957, he fell ill with inflamed lungs. He got very sick and nearly died. After recovering, Bergoglio decided to join the Society of Jesus. The Society of Jesus is a group of Roman Catholic priests. Its members are called Jesuits. They are known for their dedication to education and charity. Becoming a Jesuit priest can require more than 10 years of training. But Bergoglio was eager to learn.

CHAPTER 4

BECOMING POPE

Bergoglio finished training to become a Jesuit in 1960. In the years that followed, he slowly gained higher positions in the Church. From 1973 to 1979, he served as the top leader of the Jesuits in Argentina. In 1998, he became the **archbishop** of Buenos Aires, Argentina. And in 2001, Pope John Paul II made Bergoglio a cardinal. When Pope John Paul II died in 2005, Bergoglio was part of the group that met to elect a new pope.

Bergoglio meets with Pope John Paul II (left) in 1998.

▲ After selecting a new pope, the cardinals come out to the basilica's balcony to greet crowds.

The Catholic Church has used the same process to elect the pope for approximately 800 years. Cardinals who are less than 80 years old meet in the Sistine Chapel. They make a vow of secrecy and report to the chapel each day until they elect a new pope.

To be considered, candidates must be male and Roman Catholic. They can come from any country and be any age. However, it's very rare for a non-European to become pope. And every pope chosen since 1378 has been a cardinal.

Bergoglio was a candidate in the 2005 election. But he came in second, and the position went to Pope Benedict XVI instead. However, only eight years later, Pope Benedict XVI surprised the world by resigning. The elderly pope's health was failing. He was the first pope to resign in 600 years.

In March 2013, the cardinals gathered in the Sistine Chapel for another election. Bergoglio was a candidate in this election as well. This time, however, he was not expected to win. At age 76, Bergoglio was older than most people thought the new pope would be. Many Catholics assumed the new pope would be between 50 and 60 years old.

They wanted a pope who could lead the Church for many years.

Inside the Sistine Chapel, the cardinals began the voting process. To become pope, a candidate must receive two-thirds of the votes. Cardinals take part in multiple rounds of voting until they can make a clear selection. After each round, a cardinal burns the ballots. Outside, people watch the chapel's chimney. If black smoke comes out, a pope has not yet been chosen. White smoke means the cardinals have made a decision.

The voting process can take days, weeks, or even years. Many rounds can end in black smoke. But in 2013, the selection was clear after only five rounds. On the second day of voting, Bergoglio received more than 90 of 115 votes. According to one cardinal, it was an emotional moment. He said there wasn't a dry eye in the room.

In 2013, Pope Francis's election made headlines around the world.

Once elected, every pope chooses an official name. Bergoglio chose to be called Pope Francis. This name honored St. Francis of Assisi. He was a saint from the 1200s who gave up his wealth to live with the poor. Pope Francis was the first pope to take the name of this saint. He was also the first pope from the Americas and the first Jesuit pope. Pope Francis had just been elected, yet he was already breaking tradition.

CHAPTER 5

CHANGING THE CHURCH

Pope Francis continued making changes during his first months as pope. One change was his housing. Usually, the pope lives in the Apostolic Palace in Vatican City. But Pope Francis chose to live in the Vatican guesthouse. This building was smaller and less fancy. Another change happened during Holy Week, the week between Palm Sunday and Easter on the Christian calendar. Most popes held Mass at a church in Rome during this time.

Pope Francis began a tradition of washing the feet of inmates during Holy Week.

But Pope Francis visited a prison. He showed compassion for inmates by washing their feet. In the Bible, Jesus washed the feet of his followers. This act was a symbol of humility. By copying it, Pope Francis showed his desire to be humble, too.

Pope Francis has worked to make the Church more inclusive, or welcoming to all kinds of people. In 2013, a reporter asked him a question about **homosexuality**. Pope Francis responded that it was not his place to judge people who are gay. This response was very different from what other popes have said. The Catholic Church believes that taking part in homosexual acts is a **sin**. But Pope Francis thinks Christians should love and include gay people in the Church.

Pope Francis also wants to include people who have been divorced. In April 2016, he released a document about family life. The document was

The Catholic Church has rules regarding who can receive communion.

called "The Joy of Love." Part of it suggested that divorced or remarried couples should be able to receive **communion**. This goes against traditional Catholic belief, which states that divorce is a sin.

Furthermore, Pope Francis made 2016 a Jubilee Year. This is a time when Catholics focus on the theme of mercy. The Catholic Church held the first Jubilee Year in 1300. Since then, Jubilee Years are usually celebrated every 25 to 50 years.

No one expected a Jubilee Year in 2016. But Pope Francis wanted to remind the Church of the importance of mercy.

Pope Francis has faced several challenges. One is **corruption** in the Church. Pope Francis has tried to reduce this corruption. An example is his work in the Vatican bank. The pope has worked to make this secretive bank more open with its information. He closed thousands of unnecessary accounts. He also required people outside the bank to check its finances regularly.

The biggest challenge is child sex abuse. According to a 2004 report, more than 4,000 US priests were accused of abusing children in the last 50 years. Priests in countries around the world faced similar charges. This serious problem left many people shocked and angry. Pope Francis set up a group to address the issue. However, two

⬥ As part of spreading his message of compassion, Pope Francis works with other religious leaders.

former victims of sex abuse have left the group. They said the Church was not open to change.

Pope Francis has worked to spread a message of compassion and love. In some cases, he has acted on that message. However, he has many critics. They say he has done very little to stop child sex abuse. Although Pope Francis has made change, his critics argue that he has not done enough.

CHAPTER 6

CHANGING THE WORLD

Pope Francis takes an active role in politics. As head of the Catholic Church, he has power to influence other world leaders. He also leads the Vatican, which is the government of Vatican City. Vatican City has political relationships with more than 180 nations. And it can attend meetings of the United Nations (UN). This organization promotes cooperation among many countries around the world.

Pope Francis visited Havana, Cuba, in 2015. He rode a vehicle known as the popemobile.

Pope Francis meets with the president of Ukraine in 2015.

Pope Francis often works to resolve conflicts. One example is the tension between the United States and Cuba. In the 1950s, the United States helped a dictator gain power in Cuba. But Cuban leader Fidel Castro overthrew him. Once in power, Castro raised taxes on US goods. US leaders responded by restricting trade and travel with Cuba. Their relationship stayed tense for years.

In 2014, Pope Francis sent letters to Cuban President Raúl Castro and US President Barack Obama. He urged them to make peace. He also hosted a meeting between the two nations. With the pope's support, they made a deal. They agreed to reopen **embassies** in each other's capitals. However, the deal was threatened in 2017. That year, Donald Trump became the US president and reversed many of Obama's actions.

Pope Francis has also tried to help Israel and Palestine. These nations have been fighting for the same area of land since 1948. Pope Francis hopes a two-state solution will bring peace. In this plan, both nations would be independent countries. Each would control part of the land. The Vatican officially recognized Palestine as independent in 2015. But this move hurt the Vatican's relationship with Israel.

▲ Palestine's President Mahmoud Abbas (left) and Israel's President Shimon Peres (right) meet with Pope Francis.

Both Israel and Palestine claim the city of Jerusalem as their capital. In December 2017, President Trump announced that the United States recognized Jerusalem as the capital of Israel. Many world leaders, including the pope, disagreed with Trump's decision. They thought it would make the conflict worse. Pope Francis spoke out more than once after Trump's decision. He urged world leaders not to stir up conflict.

Pope Francis has taken stances on other global issues as well. In 2015, he wrote a letter calling on people to take better care of the planet. In 2018, he met with leaders of some of the world's largest oil companies. They talked about ways to fight **climate change**.

The pope has also addressed the world's migrant crisis. In August 2017, he released a 20-point plan. The plan described actions that countries can take to help migrants. Pope Francis has even offered Vatican housing to several migrant families from Syria.

THINK ABOUT IT ◁

As a religious leader, the pope has a unique role in world politics. What advantages does this role give him? Can you think of any disadvantages?

FOCUS ON

BARTHOLOMEW I

Patriarch Bartholomew I is the 270th leader of the Eastern Orthodox Church. The Roman Catholic Church and the Eastern Orthodox Church have a long, rocky history. In the early centuries of Christianity, the churches were united. But in 1054 CE, they split apart. The churches disagreed about the role of the pope. They also held different views on other religious beliefs. For many years, the churches had a very strained relationship.

Bartholomew I and Pope Francis want to mend this relationship. Instead of focusing on differences, the leaders have come together to act on issues they both care about. For example, Pope Francis hosted Bartholomew I at the Vatican in 2014. Together, they prayed for peace between Israel and Palestine. And in 2017, the

▲ Patriarch Bartholomew I has been the leader of the Eastern Orthodox Church since 1991.

leaders shared a message with the world about climate change.

Both men lead huge groups of people. Roughly 1.2 billion people around the world are Catholics. And approximately 300 million people belong to the Orthodox Church. By working together, the two leaders can reach more people.

CHAPTER 7

THE FUTURE OF THE CHURCH

At first, Pope Francis enjoyed widespread popularity. He inspired crowds with his message of mercy and compassion. Catholics around the world approved of him. So did many non-Catholics. Within two years, however, his approval ratings had begun to fall. For example, 76 percent of people in the United States said they approved of Pope Francis in 2014. That number had dropped to 59 percent by 2015.

Pope Francis greets a crowd during his weekly meeting with the public in St. Peter's Square.

The pope's critics come from more than one political group. Some people think he needs to be more open-minded on social topics. They think he hasn't done enough to help people who have been hurt by the Church. Other critics think the pope is rejecting the Church's traditional values. They fear he is too open-minded about topics such as

➤ THE POPE'S IMPACT

Responses of US Catholics when asked how Pope Francis has affected the Catholic Church:

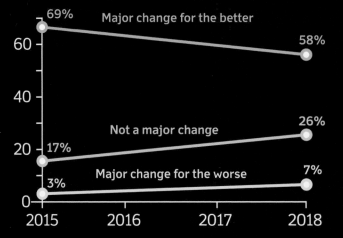

Note: Figures do not add up to 100% due to additional responses not shown and/or rounding.

divorce and immigration. In addition, people from both groups criticize his lack of response to child sex abuse. Some even accused him of covering up this serious problem.

Low attendance has been another ongoing problem for the Catholic Church. Attendance has been falling since the 1950s. The pope's supporters say he has helped bring more people to the Catholic Church, but a 2018 survey showed no increase in church attendance since 2013. Pope Francis did not cause these problems, but both issues place pressure on him as the Church's leader. Many Catholics look to him to keep the Church alive.

THINK ABOUT IT ◁

Do you think approval ratings are a good way to measure a pope's success? Why or why not?

FOCUS ON
POPE FRANCIS

Write your answers on a separate piece of paper.

1. Write a paragraph describing the process used for electing the pope.

2. Do you think Pope Francis brought positive change to the Catholic Church? Why or why not?

3. In what country was Pope Francis born?
    A. Argentina
    B. Italy
    C. Palestine

4. In 2013, how did people outside the Sistine Chapel learn that a new pope was elected?
    A. White smoke came out of the chimney.
    B. Black smoke came out of the chimney.
    C. Smoke stopped coming out the chimney.

Answer key on page 48.

GLOSSARY

archbishop
A leader who oversees all the bishops in a larger region.

bishop
A leader who oversees a local region of the Catholic Church.

climate change
A long-term change in Earth's temperature and weather patterns.

communion
The act of sharing bread and wine at a Christian worship service.

confession
The act of admitting wrongdoings to a Catholic priest.

corruption
Dishonest or illegal acts, especially by powerful people.

delegates
Assigns tasks or responsibilities to another person, usually someone with less power.

embassies
Buildings where representatives from another country live or work.

homosexuality
Sexual attraction between members of the same gender.

migrants
People who attempt to permanently move to a new country.

seminary
A school people attend to become priests, rabbis, or ministers.

sin
An action that goes against a set of religious beliefs.

TO LEARN MORE

BOOKS

Gormley, Beatrice. *Pope Francis*. New York: Aladdin, 2017.

Marsico, Katie. *Christianity*. Ann Arbor, MI: Cherry Lake Publishing, 2017.

Spinner, Stephanie. *Who Is Pope Francis?* New York: Penguin Workshop, 2017.

NOTE TO EDUCATORS

Visit **www.focusreaders.com** to find lesson plans, activities, links, and other resources related to this title.

INDEX

Answer Key: 1. Answers will vary; **2.** Answers will vary; **3.** A; **4.** A